JHM →
WITH ALL MY LOVE
ON YOUR 25TH.
BR

NIGHTS IN

A FIRESIDE BOOK ▼ PUBLISHED BY

BIRDLAND

JAZZ PHOTOGRAPHS 1954 · 1960

WITH AN ESSAY BY JACK KEROUAC

CAROLE REIFF

SIMON & SCHUSTER, INC. ▼ NEW YORK

COPYRIGHT © 1985, 1987 BY HAL & FLORENCE REIFF
ALL RIGHTS RESERVED
INCLUDING THE RIGHT OF REPRODUCTION
IN WHOLE OR IN PART IN ANY FORM
A FIRESIDE BOOK,
PUBLISHED BY SIMON & SCHUSTER, INC.
SIMON & SCHUSTER BUILDING
ROCKEFELLER CENTER
1230 AVENUE OF THE AMERICAS
NEW YORK, NEW YORK 10020
FIRESIDE AND COLOPHON ARE REGISTERED
TRADEMARKS OF SIMON & SCHUSTER, INC.

DESIGNED BY BONNI LEON

MANUFACTURED IN THE UNITED STATES OF AMERICA
10 9 8 7 6 5 4 3 2 1
ISBN: 0-671-63281-7

A NOTE ON THE CAPTIONS:
EVERY EFFORT HAS BEEN MADE TO IDENTIFY THE MUSICIANS IN THESE
PHOTOGRAPHS. MANY OF THE PHOTOGRAPHER'S NEGATIVES AND PROOF
SHEETS WERE UNMARKED, HOWEVER, AND POSITIVE IDENTIFICATION
OF PEOPLE, PLACES, AND DATES COULD NOT ALWAYS BE MADE.

A C K N O W L E D G M E N T S

f I had not known it was Carole's wish to see her photographs published, I would not have been driven to complete her task. I thank her for the beautiful legacy she has left.

Many thanks to the artists who appear within the pages of this book.

I AM GRATEFUL TO: Ivy Fischer Stone for her sensitivity and support. Fifi Oscard for her cooperation. Tim McGinnis, editor, for his love of jazz and for making the book possible. Hal Reiff, her mentor. John Iozia, for his archival assistance. Peter Osnato for his friendship. Ellis Simberloff, her devoted companion. Harry, her dog, who never chewed up a photograph.

—FLORENCE REIFF

THE BEGINNING OF BOP

BY JACK KEROUAC

Bop began with jazz but one afternoon somewhere on a sidewalk maybe 1939, 1940, Dizzy Gillespie or Charley Parker or Thelonious Monk was walking down past a men's clothing store on 42nd Street or South Main in L.A. and from the loudspeaker they suddenly heard a wild impossible mistake in jazz that could only have been heard inside their own imaginary head, and that is a new art. Bop. The name derives from an accident, America was named after an Italian explorer and not after an Indian king. Lionel Hampton had made a record called "Hey Baba Ree Bop" and everybody yelled it and it was when Lionel would jump in the audience and whale his saxophone at everybody with sweat, claps, jumping fools in the aisles, the drummer booming and belaboring on his stage as the whole theater rocked. Sung by Helen Humes it was a popular record and sold many copies in 1945, 1946. First everyone looked around then it happened—bop happened—the bird flew in—minds went in—on the streets thousands of new-type hepcats in red shirts and some goatees and strange queerlooking cowboys from the West with boots and belts, and the girls began to disappear from the street— you no longer saw as in the Thirties the wrangler walking with his doll in the honkytonk, now he was alone, rebop, bop, came into being because the broads were leaving the guys and going off to be middleclass models. Dizzy or Charley or Thelonious was walking down the street, heard a noise, a sound, half Lester Young, half raw-rainy-fog that has that chest-shivering excitement of shack, track, empty lot, the sudden vast Tiger head on the woodfence rainy no-school Saturday morning dumpyards, "Hey!" and rushed off dancing.

On the piano that night Thelonious introduced a wooden off-key note to everybody's warmup notes, Minton's Playhouse, evening starts, jam hours later, 10 P.M., colored bar and hotel next door, one or two white visitors some from Columbia some from Nowhere—some from ships—some from Army Navy Air Force Marines—some from Europe—The strange note makes the trumpeter of the band lift an eyebrow. Dizzy is surprised for the first time that day. He puts the trumpet to lips and blows a wet blur—

"Hee ha ha!" laughs Charley Parker bending down to slap his ankle. He puts his alto to his mouth and says "Didn't I tell you?"—with jazz of notes . . . Talking eloquent like great poets of foreign languages singing in foreign countries with lyres, by seas, and no one understands because the language isn't alive in the land yet—Bop is the language from America's inevitable Africa, *going* is sounded like *gong*, Africa is the name of the flue and kick beat, off to one side—the sudden squeak uninhibited that screams muffled at any moment from Dizzy Gillespie's trumpet —do anything you want—drawing the tune aside along another improvisation bridge with a reach-out tear of claws, why be subtle and false?

The band of 10 P M Minton's swings into action, Bird Parker who is only 18 year old has a crew cut of Africa looks impossible has perfect eyes and composures of a king when suddenly you stop and look at him in the subway and you can't believe that bop is here to stay—that it is real, Negroes in America are just like us, we must look at them understanding the exact racial counterpart of what the man is—and figure it with histories and lost kings of immemorial tribes in jungle and Fellaheen town and otherwise and the sad mutts sleeping on old porches in Big Easonburg woods where just 90 years ago old Roost came running calling "Maw" through the fence he'd just deserted the Confederate Army and was running home for pone—and flies on watermelon porches. And educated judges in horn-rimmed glasses reading the Amsterdam News.

The band realized the goof of life that had made them be not only misplaced in a white nation but mis-noticed for what they really were and the goof they felt stirring and springing in their bellies, suddenly Dizzy spats his lips tight-drum together and drives a high screeching fantastic clear note that has everybody in the joint look up—Bird, lips hanging dully to hear, is turning slowly in a circle waiting for Diz to swim through the wave of the tune in a toneless complicated wave of his own grim like factories and atonal at any minute and the logic of the mad, the sock in his belly is sweet, the rock, zonga, monga, bang—In white creamed afternoons of blue Bird had leaned back dreamily in eternity as Dizzy outlined to him the importance of becoming Mohammedans in order to give a solid basis of *race* to their ceremony, "Make that rug swing, mother,—When you say Race bow your head and close your eyes." Give them a religion no Uncle Tom Baptist—make them wearers of skull caps of respectable minarets in actual New York—picking hashi dates from their teeth—Give them new names with zonga sounds—make it weird—

Thelonious was so weird he wandered the twilight streets of Harlem in winter with no hat on his hair, sweating, blowing fog—In his head he heard it all ringing. Often he heard whole choruses by Lester. There was a strange English kid hanging around Minton's who stumbled along the sidewalk hearing Lester in his head too—hours of hundreds of developing choruses in regular beat all day so in the subway no dissonance could crash against unalterable choruses in implacable bars—erected in mind's foundation jazz.

The tune they were playing was *All the Things You Are* . . . they slowed it down and dragged behind it at half tempo dinosaur proportions—changed the placing of the note in the middle of the harmony to an outer more precarious position where also its sense of not belonging was enhanced by the general atonality produced with everyone exteriorizing the tune's harmony, the clonk of the millenial piano like anvils in Petrograd—"Blow!" said Diz, and Charley Parker came in for his solo with a squeaky innocent cry. Monk punched anguished nub fingers crawling at the keyboard to tear up foundations and guts of jazz from the big masterbox, to make Charley Parker hear his cry and sigh—to jar the orchestra into vibrations—to elicit gloom from the doom of the black piano. He stared down wild eyed at his keys like a matador at the bull's head. Groan. Drunken figures shaded in the weaving background, tottering—the boys didn't care. On cold corners they stood three backs to one another, facing all the winds, bent—lips don't care—miserable cold and broke—waiting like witchdoctors—saying, "Everything belongs to me because I am poor." Like 12 Century monks high in winter belfries of the Gothic Organ they wildeyed were listening to their own wild sound which was heralding in a new age of music that would eventually require symphonies, schools, centuries of technique, declines and falls of master-ripe styles—the Dixieland of Louis Armstrong sixteen in New Orleans and of big Pops Forest niggerlips jim in the white shirt whaling at a big scarred bass in raunchy nongry New Orleans on South Rampart street famous for parades and old Perdido Street—all that was mud in the river Mississippi, pasts of 1910 gold rings, derby hats of workers, horses steaming turds near breweries and saloons,—Soon enough it would leap and fill the gay Twenties like champagne in a glass, pop!—And crawl up to the Thirties with tired Rudy Vallees lamenting what Louis had laughed in a Twenties Transoceanic Jazz, sick and tired early Ethel Mermans, and old beat bedsprings creaking in that stormy weather blues when people lay in bed all day and moaned and had it good—The world of the United States was tired of being poor and low and gloomy in a line. Swing erupted as the Depression began to crack, it was the year marijuana was made illegal, 1937. Young teenagers took to the first restraint, the second, the third, some still wandered on hobo trains (lost boys of the Thirties numbered in the hundreds of thousands. Salvation Armies put up full houses every night and some were ten years old)—teenagers, alienated from their parents who have suddenly returned to work and for good to get rid of that dam old mud of the river—and tear the rose vine off the porch—and paint the porch white—and cut the trees down—castrate the hedges—burn the leaves—build a wire fence—get up an antenna—listen— the alienated teenager in the 20th Century finally ripe gone wild modern to be rich and prosperous no more just around the corner—became the hepcat, the jitterbug, and smoked the new law weed. World War II gave everybody two pats of butter in the morning on a service tray, including your sister. Up from tired degrading swing wondering what happened between 1937 and 1945 and because the Army'd worked it canned it played it to the boys in North Africa and raged it in Picadilly bars and the Andrews sisters put the corn on the can—swing with its heroes died—and Charley Parker, Dizzy Gillespie and Thelonious Monk who were hustled through the chow lines —came back remembering old goofs—and tried it again—and Zop! Dizzy screamed, Charley squealed, Monk crashed, the drummer kicked, dropped a bomb—the bass questionmark plunked—and off they whaled on Salt Peanuts jumping like mad monkeys in the gray new air. "Hey Porkpie, Porkpie, Hey Porkpie!"

"Skidilibee-la-bee you,—oo,—e bop she bam, ske too ria—Parasakiliaoolza—menooriastiba-tiolyait—oon ya koo." They came into their own, they jumped, they had jazz and took it in their hands and saw its history vicissitudes and developments and turned it to their weighty use and heavily carried it clanking like posts across the enormity of a new world philosophy and a new strange and crazy grace came over them, fell from the air free, they saw pity in the hole of heaven, hell in their hearts, Billy Holliday had rocks in her heart, Lester droopy porkpied hung his horn and blew bop lazy ideas inside jazz had everybody dreaming (Miles Davis leaning against the piano fingering his trumpet with a cigarette hand working making raw iron sound like wood speaking in long sentences like Marcel Proust)—"Hey Jim," and the stud comes swinging down the street and says he's real *bent* and he's *down* and he has a *twisted* face, he works, he wails, he bops, he bangs, this man who was sent, stoned and stabbed is now *down, bent* and *stretched-out* —he is home at last, his music is here to stay, his history has washed over us, his imperialistic kingdoms are coming.

—*Escapade*, April 1959

NIGHTS IN BIRDLAND

Cannonball Adderley,   **Stan Getz,**

Al Cohn,   Junior Cook.

B

illie Holiday, backstage at the Lady Sings the Blues concert, Carnegie Hall, October 1956.

Left: Louis Armstrong, Basin Street

West, New York City, April 1954.   Above: Ray Charles.

ouis Armstrong, Basin Street West, New York City, April 1954.

Above: four women sing-
ers. Right: Art Blakey,
the Apollo Theater, New
York City, 1959.

J unior Cook,

Ames Studio,

New York City,

September 1958.

Willie Dennis.

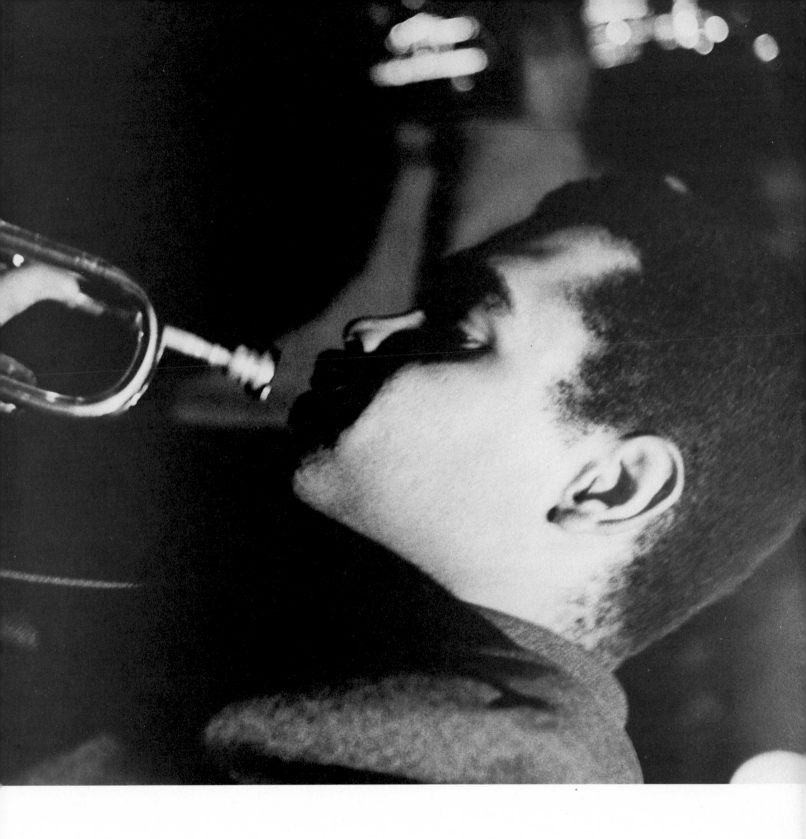

Art Farmer.

Overleaf: Sonny Rollins.

Above: Art Blakey.

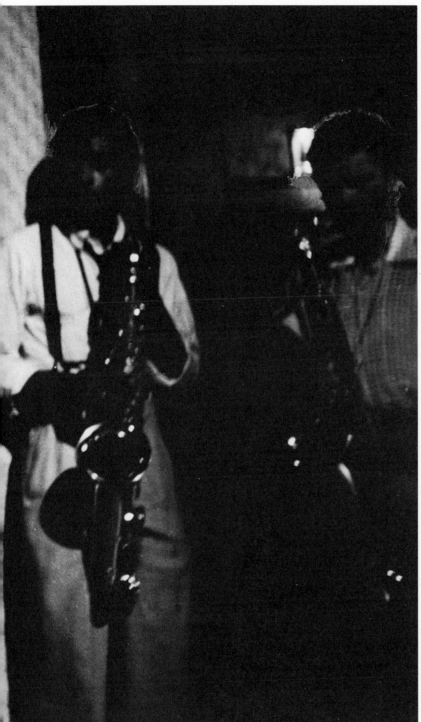

Chet Baker,
The Open Door,
New York City,
July 1955.

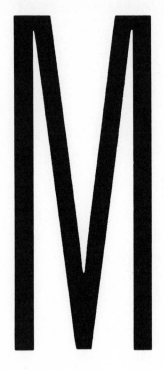**M**iles Davis
(with George
Avakian,
upper right),
Columbia
recording
session.

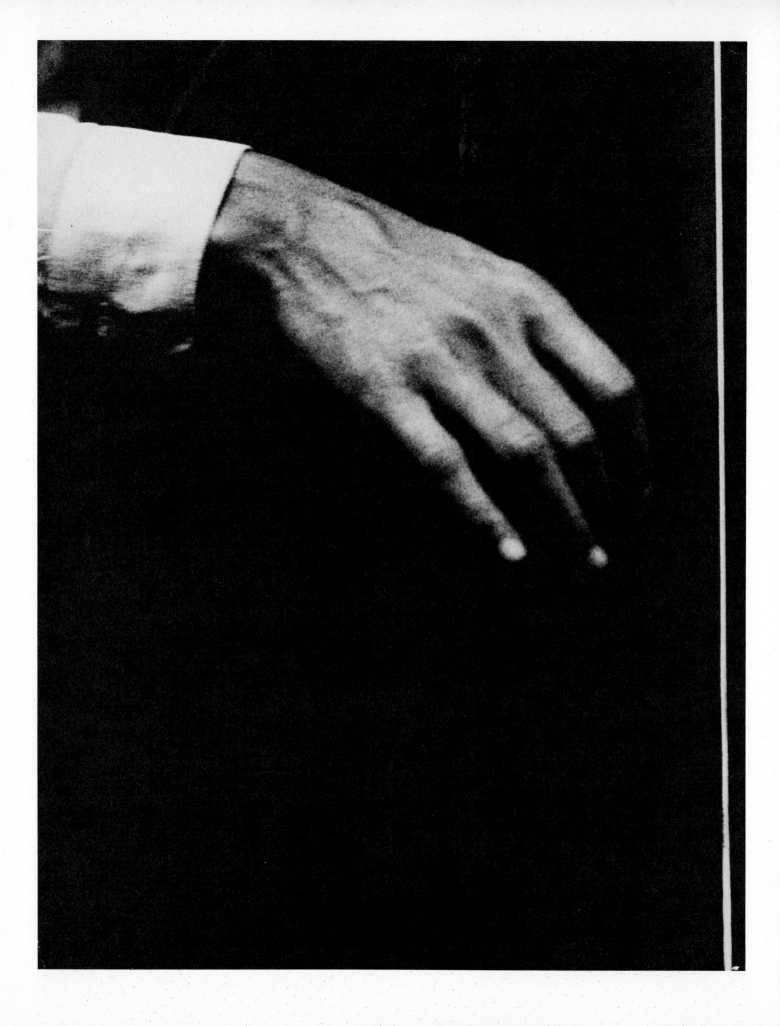

R ashaan Roland Kirk, with Ahmad Jamal at the piano, Chicago, 1960.

Ray Charles and Dinah Washington, Soul '60, Chicago, 1960.

J ohn
Coltrane.

Left to

right:

Billy Taylor,

1955;

Bud Powell,

New York

City, 1955;

and

Count Basie,

Town Hall,

New York City.

Bob Maltz,

Hazel Scott,

and Duke

Ellington,

Town Hall,

New York

City, 1960.

E

lla Fitzgerald, August 1955.

B ud Powell.

Gil Evans in concert.

D izzy Gillespie, Argo Studios, Chicago, 1960.

Overleaf: Left: unidentified.

Right: Al Cohn (left), Zoot Sims.

Dinah Washington, the Apollo Theater, New York City, 1959. Left: Gil Evans.

H

orace Silver and band, Ames Studio, September 1958: Louis Hayes on drums, Gene Taylor on bass, Junior Cook on sax, trumpeter unidentified.

Lee Morgan (foreground), Wayne Shorter.

Lucky Thompson, 1956.

B obby Timmons.

E
lvin Jones.

Al Cohn.

Paul Chambers.

H

orace Silver.

Jimmy Raney.

Bill Evans (left), unidentified.

Left: Zoot Sims. Above: Teddy Kotick (right), unidentified.

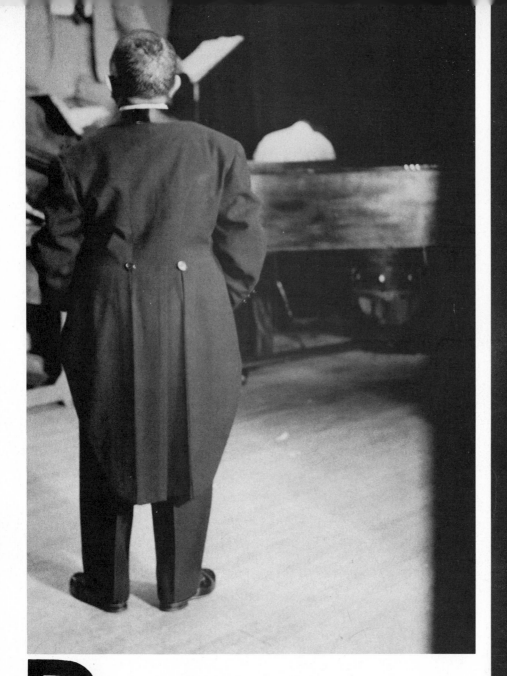

P ee Wee Marquet, the doorman at Birdland.

Art Blakey.

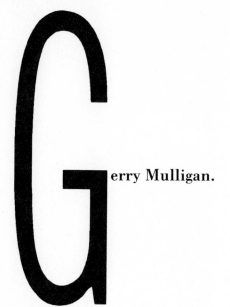erry Mulligan.

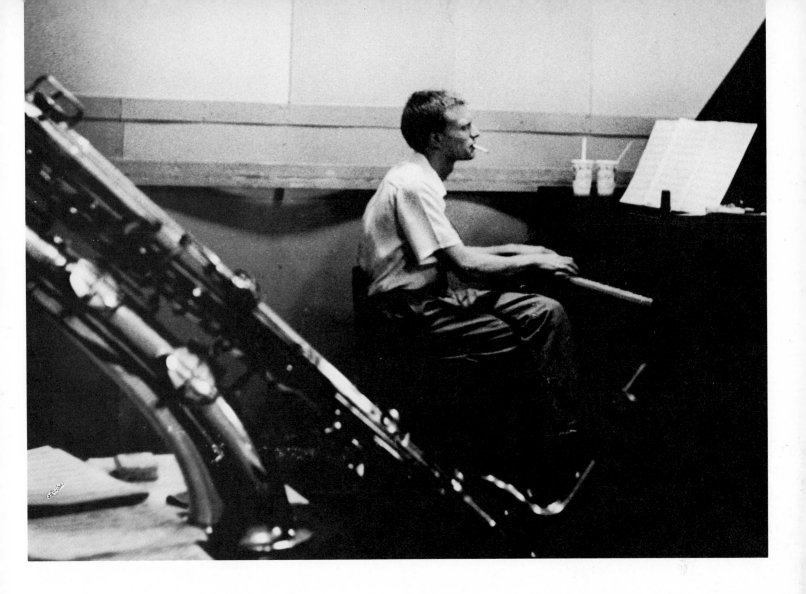

Billie Holiday, backstage at Carnegie Hall, October 10, 1956.

Above: Cannonball Adderley.   Right: Gigi Gryce.

J

ohn Coltrane, Town Hall, New York City.

Above: Lester Young.

Overleaf: Donald Byrd and band, Washington Square, New York City.

R

ay Charles,

Chicago,

1960.

rnette

Coleman,

Music Inn,

Lenox,

Mass.,

June 1959.

Above:
Lionel Hampton,
Westchester
County Center,
April 1955.
Right: Count
Basie,
Birdland,
February 1955.

Left: Jimmy Giuffre.   Above: unidentified.

M ax Roach.

R

ay Charles and Dinah
Washington, Soul '60, Chicago, 1960.

Billie Holiday,
rehearsing at
Carnegie Hall,
1956.

Left: Bobby Hackett.   Above: unidentified.

Overleaf: Left: Sarah Vaughan, Birdland concert, Carnegie Hall. Right: Johnny Hodges.

Joe Williams, July 1955.

Right: Gil Evans.

Unidentified.

Johnny

Hodges

(with Duke

Ellington

in the

background);

Sonny Stitt;

both at

Basin

Street

West,

New York

City, 1956.

Stan Getz.

Sonny Stitt.

Charles Mingus on the "Steve Allen Show," Nov. 17, 1956.

Left: unidentified.   Above: Jackie McLean.

Thelonious Monk, 1955.

Overleaf: Left: unidentified.   Right: Percy Heath.

E

lvin Jones.

Freddie Green, Randall's Island, New York City, August 1956.

H ank Jones.

Carole Reiff.

ABOUT THE PHOTOGRAPHER

Carole Reiff graduated from the High School of Music and Art in New York City and studied at the Art Students League and the Museum of Modern Art's Peoples Art Center. In 1954, she began to photograph jazz musicians. As a free-lance photojournalist, she covered recording sessions, interviews, jam sessions, events, and concerts for record companies—Columbia, Atlantic, Riverside, United Artists, and Prestige, among others. Her photographs appeared in *Esquire, Time*, and the trade journals. *Metronome* magazine cited her portrait of Thelonious Monk as "Jazz Photograph of the Year, 1956." She was Photographer-in-Residence at the School of Jazz at Music Inn in Lenox, Massachusetts, and her photographs of John Coltrane and Billie Holiday are in the permanent collection of the New York Jazz Museum. Carole Reiff died in 1984.